07032015

The Starter Home*

Volume One

Positioning

The starter home* project began with a question – how could an architecture office, OJT, and and a developer, Charles Rutledge, not only share expertise and in so doing create a streamlined, vertically integrated design-development system, but more broadly, how could we collectively respond to what we perceive as a gap in the market with a spatial logic – one that would rely not only on an innovative view of land markets, regulatory processes, and capital and equity access, but would take a distinctly opportunistic view of the totality of the design-develop process.

As an architecture office, we aspire to participate in the evolution of the typology, to create housing that not only reflects the present moment, but is also simultaneously prescient and aspirational. To design a domestic environment is to have a thesis about domesticity, and we feel that a domestic argument should reflect not only patterns of every-day use, but the ideological, psychological, socio-economic, political constructions implied thereby.

The work in this series of books represents some of the many and myriad inquiries that our office has undertaken as part of our exploration of the "starter home," and our construction of our own starter home* argument. What began as a conversation has been absorbed into the office milieu as a shared, progressively evolving obsession. The following is by no means meant to be comprehensive, but rather implicative of an ongoing investigation.

Editors

Rebecca Fitzgerald
Jonathan Tate

Project Team

Robert Baddour
Travis Bost
Rebecca Fitzgerald
Kristian Mizes
Charles Rutledge
Jonathan Tate

The Starter Home*, Vol I.

Distributed by OJT:
www.officejt.com

All attempts have been made
to trace and acknowledge the
sources of images and data.
Regarding any omissions or
errors, interested parties are
requested to contact Office
of Jonathan Tate, c/o Starter
Home*, 1336 Magazine
St. Suite 1, New Orleans,
Louisiana 70130.

Unless specifically
referenced all photographs
and graphic work by
Authors.

fig. 001

James Casabere's "Landscape with Houses",
2011

Contents

The Burden of Cyclical Certainty

Holes in the City, Cracks in the Market

Strategy & Form

Place & Place-lessness

The Burden of Cyclical Certainty

fig. 002

**James Casabere's "Landscape with Houses",
2011**

The economic linch-pin

fig. 003

Home Owners' financing brochure, 1920

"Home reflects character. More, it moulds character. Home is the image of thought, exposed, inviting the gaze of the world. As your home is, so are you."

Currency, indicator, and industry

There is no more resonant product of 20th century America than that of the "starter home," the symbolic and realized entry of a consumer into the housing market and by extension, the broader economy; the ascendancy of ownership in the American mythology has, over the past 100 years or so, defined our understanding of what it means to be socially mobile, financially secure, civic-minded, and fully participatory in a particular national ideology.

The "starter home," as a type, has developed according to a series of metrics, each of which has had its major moment of relevance as new ideologies and technologies effect change on the domestic landscape. Whatever their differences, starter homes share a mutual genesis as responses to a need for housing, the desire to attract new consumers to the housing market and the economy at large, and often, an attraction on the part of the designer, planner, and/or architect to participate in the broader typology and in so doing, propose new architectural models of domestic inhabitation. The starter home's efficacy as a way to draw new consumers into the housing market has long been associated with a progression towards replicable forms, large-lot subdivision, and lower delivery costs, just as its ability to frame the ideological and socio-political argument for domesticity has been guided in the direction of individual self-sustainability from the scale of the home to that of the planned community.

A house with a future

fig. 004

Segmental House, 1942

fig. 005

Fortune magazine cover showing Eichler's Palo Alto Fairmeadow subdivision, 1955

tune
The Burden of Cyclical Certainty

ry 1955

ifth Anniversary Year

5., 1930-55   *What Caused the Depression?*

Rockefeller Brothers   *The Cadillac Craze*

And twenty other timely articles — see page 1

A capitalist marriage – governing industry:

By the 1930s, the relationship of the single-family, especially starter, home industry, the federal government, and the national economy was such that "suburban residential fabric [had become] a currency, an economic indicator, and major U.S. industry not unlike the automobile." [01] The point at which the housing industry, and moreover the starter home industry, became inextricably linked to the overall presumption of national economic health can be traced to the National Housing Act of 1934, when the Federal Housing Authority was created, and a system through which, significantly, the government insured banks rather than mortgage holders, codified housing as the United States' most significant commodity. Though an ideology that defined the centrality of domesticity in the proper functioning of the nation was already well ingrained in the American imaginary by the 1920s, the connection between overall economic health and the pressure to build new homes had not yet been systematized until the FHA was established.

01

Keller Easterling's Call it Home: The House that Private Enterprise Built

The home, and everything in it, is positioned as America's most essential economic driver...

"Glorifying the American Housewife"
By Neysa McMein

A series by famous artists; courtesy B. T. Babbitt & Co.

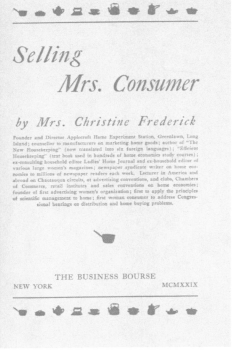

Selling
Mrs. Consumer

by Mrs. Christine Frederick

Founder and Director Applecroft Home Experiment Station, Greenlawn, Long Island; counsellor to manufacturers on marketing home goods; author of "The New Housekeeping" (now translated into six foreign languages); "Efficient Housekeeping" (text book used in hundreds of home economics study courses); ex-consulting household editor Ladies' Home Journal and ex-household editor of various large women's magazines; newspaper syndicate writer on home economies to millions of newspaper readers each week. Lecturer in America and abroad on Chautauqua circuits, at advertising conventions, and clubs, Chambers of Commerce, retail institutes and sales conventions on home economies; founder of first advertising women's organization; first to apply the principles of scientific management to home; first woman consumer to address Congressional hearings on distribution and home buying problems.

THE BUSINESS BOURSE
NEW YORK   MCMXXIX

To
HERBERT HOOVER

more packaged food, bakery goods, tea and coffee. We spend 11¼ cents of the consumer's dollar for automobiles, 4½ cents on tobacco. The entire toilet goods field has moved up rapidly, the per capita consumption (calculated on wholesale value) being now about $1.75. It was $1.50 at the last (1927) census.

BUDGET FIGURES SHOWING INCREASE SINCE 1913

Education is another "luxury" that is gaining rapidly—as is radio, amusements, sports, travel, etc. Ice cream, soft drinks, restaurant eating, smart shoes for women, furs, jewels, etc., are all showing decided upward trends. Even chewing gum grows and grows! More service of all kinds is bought than ever before. The steam laundries have multiplied their volume by five in 16 years. Their 600 million dollar 1928

37

fig. 006

**Spreads from Christine Frederick's
"Selling Mrs. Consumer" 1929**

After World War II, as the Federal Housing Act of 1949 joined the post-war imperative to redirect resources – material and ideological – towards the single-family, starter home industry to fuel an already massive industry to new heights. In the 1950s, American housing stock grew by 27%, a rate of growth overcome in the 1970s, with a 29% increase over the decade. [02] New construction has consistently dominated by the single-family home, with major advertising and lending efforts directed towards first-time-homeowners.

Cycles in the housing market have necessarily been matched by broader economic up and downturns. During the years leading up to the most recent housing market crash, a trend building since the 1970s became fully manifest: access to capital was increasingly emphasized over access to homes, abstracting the mortgage lending process and divorcing product from use. Zoning regulations that set minimum lot and home dimensions exacerbated a historical condition that had polarized the nation's land market and helped to force the price of housing up absent an increase in actual, or use-based, home value. This matrix of conditions fed the assumption that a large home is necessary both for the individual's investment return and for the neighborhood's socio-economic stability. Market collapse was therefore predicated, in part, on two equally powerful forces: regulated access – social, financial, geographic – and deregulated lending.

A crisis of confidence, reframing expectations:

The consequences of economic downturns cannot be overstated, especially in arenas less measurable: collective views of investment, property ownership, financial security and mobility. A third, incredibly potent force has been implicated in the collapse of the American housing industry and its subsequently reticent recovery: the ideology of home ownership itself. The future of the starter home in America is indistinct; an inchoate idea of imminent change, exacerbated by lingering post-recession conditions, guides our discussions, but we are as yet unsure if we are amending the wages of sin, requiring a radical paradigm shift – a counter-myth – or repackaging a functional but stylistically outdated model for a new generation's consumption. We are experiencing a crisis both of housing affordability and of housing ideology: public funding,

Kent Colton's "Housing in the 21st Century"

mortgage financing, banking regulation and urban sprawl are among some of the major issues coming to a head in both the public and private spheres.

Of course, redefining the American Dream sans homeownership is one path forward; to productively engage the logic embedded in the evolution of the starter home, on the other hand, requires something other than altered rhetoric. The Starter Home* asks, Can we apply a functional ideal to a new model: one that operates beyond superficial associations and the strictures of expectations of material constancy, and embraces the value in its own systematic functioning? It is a strategic model, with a tactical architecture – one based in the market as much as it is in a progressive conceptual framing – that is required in order to address the typological and economic stagnation we find in the condition of the contemporary American starter home.

From 1977-1980, interest rates increased by 58%, directly affecting interest-sensitive industries – housing and auto; a restructuring of the housing industry according to debt accumulation and debt trading followed.

fig. 008

Flint, MI 1964

The legacy of single-use zoning is especially evident in America's shrinking cities.

fig. 009

Portland, Oregon 1974

fig. 007

"Broken Houses", Ofra Lapid 2010-2011

Entry-thresholds

Cost

Irrespective of market instability, home prices are prohibitively high for much of the first-time homebuyer market, especially in metropolitan areas where transportation costs are typically more affordable. This phenomenon encourages the century-old trend in the starter home market, wherein the only affordable options involve large subdivided green-field developments, far from the kinds of networks that would benefit a new homeowner with respect to the long-term affordability of his or her mortgage.

Risk

As land costs increase, intensifying associated risk encourages the expectation of high returns on real estate investments, both for the lender and the homeowner. Wavering faith in the security offered by home ownership, combined with the extreme instability of home values, especially in non-metro contexts, has created a shared mistrust of value in the housing market in general. It therefore becomes increasingly unlikely for first-time homebuyers to both feel prepared to take on a mortgage, and able to secure funding.

Capital

Because housing is both an investment good and a consumption good, volatility in the broader market affects both tenure and reinvestment at the level of the individual homeowner; on average, low-valued homes, often the only houses available to low-income borrowers, are more volatile because of their relative liquidity. This means that the more desirable investments – the higher-valued homes – are not available to an ever-broader portion of the American public, restricting access to the benefits of equity.

Lot size

Planning systems, and specifically those related to parcel geometries, help to restrict access and opportunity in turn: with Village of Euclid v. Ambler Realty Co. (1926) came the codification of an attitude toward stability in the housing market that relied on the assumption that single-use neighborhoods with regulated lot and home sizes ensured the most consistently robust returns on investments. Protecting property values and investment returns came to be indissolubly linked to homogenous single-family neighborhoods in the American imaginary, the evidence of which can be seen over the past century through selective disinvestment practices, deed restrictive covenants, neighborhood red-lining, and minimum lot dimensions. Though the discriminatory practices themselves, and the way we define

Only 16% of new home sales in 2013 were to first-time buyers - compared to a expected rate of 32% - this is attributed in part to the fact that millenials (those born roughly between 1980 and 1995) represent a significant (over 2 million) number of "missing households."

fig. 010

David Crowe, National Association of Home Builders

fig. 011

United States National Commission on Urban Problems, "Building the American City," 1969

fig. 012

US Census Bureau, "New Single-Family Homes in 2013," 2014

neighborhood desirability, have evolved over time, their purpose remains consistent: to restrict access to desirable neighborhoods to only those with access to funding.

Home size

The transition from home as consumption good to home as investment commodity at the individual level has encouraged a paradigm in which the use-value of the home for the homeowner no longer matters as much as the return on investment expected upon resale. This is an attitude that encourages overextension and often, subsequent foreclosure, in addition to a focus on the part of developers on cheaper, often less accessible, parcels where large homes can be built without incurring the high cost of metropolitan area land. The kinds of interior amenities that have become standard in these larger, less accessible homes become cheap incentives that have little to add in real value to the home itself.

Maintenance

The energy costs associated with these larger, often more cheaply constructed homes add a significant burden to the homeowner. Moreover, the cost of transportation is the second largest household expenditure after

housing, and can be anywhere from <10% to over 25% of a household's income depending on location; access to transit options and proximity to amenities can have a major effect on a household's ability to afford a home in the long-term, making a large home in an inaccessible area an even more risky purchase. Finally, the price volatility of a home – the ratio of a property's land value to the total property value – higher land leverage tends to mean greater appreciation when the housing market is strong

The median price for a single-family home remains high, in 2013 as high as $268,900; From 2009-2012, median house size increased to over 2,300 square feet—the largest since recording by the NAHB began in 1974.

fig. 013

Paul Emrath, "Characteristics of Homes Started in 2012: Size Increase Continues" NAHB, 2013

The Starter Home*

Holes in the City, Cracks in the Market

fig. 014

The Philadelphia metro area, 2008

A hybrid strategy

Between 2000 and 2009, metropolitan areas in the United States grew by 10.5%, compared to a 5.8% rate of growth in the rest of the country during that time. 84% of Americans live in metro areas, 58% commute from home to work within the same metro area, and 79% move within their metro area when they relocate.

Opportunism in development & design

Weak housing markets express themselves differently across the United States – from selective blight in otherwise well-populated neighborhoods, to completely empty housing tracts, and condo towers made over into rentals, entire neighborhoods and in some cases metropolitan areas are spatially and financially transformed when the economy falters. What has emerged from our most recent housing market collapse in many American metropolitan areas is a polarized land market – very restricted and very high value areas that are prohibitively expensive on the one hand, and large swaths of land with little to no value on the other. This is a condition that mirrors and at the same time propagates the selective post-2008 recovery seen in broader economy.

An ill-fitting model:

The 20th century development model evolved around a number of fixed expectations based on the consistency that comes with economies of scale: high rates of return, homogenous built environments and absolute control over the elements involved in the development, design and construction process, from materials to land. This model been applied in urban contexts to varying degrees of success. Because of higher land costs, these developments rely almost exclusively on market rate units – prohibitively expensive to all but the most financially stable in their respective urban areas – or a combination of market rate units for sale that subsidize more affordable rental units, which themselves are still often out of reach for many. In either case, the starter home market is all but absent from

fig. 015

Brookings Institute, "The State of Metropolitan America Report", 2010

the metropolitan areas whose resources could most directly benefit first-time homebuyers. In a metro area, where infill on lots of variable dimensions is more likely than large lot subdivision, the assumption that homogeneity is a precondition to success is the most significant impediment to urban development at scale. Once the ties that bind starter home development to homogeneity are severed, a compensatory process that requires opportunism in both development and design becomes necessary. Here, polarized metropolitan land markets, restrictive zoning regulations, and each urban landscape's particular complexities can be enlisted, guided by tactical design, to create a development strategy that is responsive enough to flourish in metro areas.

Underutilization at the city-scale:

There are many reasons that a particular lot or lot type might be deemed "un-developable," and lie fallow while surrounding lots become highly desirable investments. Among them, lot size is often a deciding factor across U.S. metro areas. The Bowman-Pagano report, a survey of vacant land across cities in the US, gives the following reasons for the underutilization of land: oversupply, undersupply, duration of vacancy, location, shape, and size. The following "test cities" were chosen for their benefit to visualizing latent potential: they are all cities with housing demands that outweigh their current offerings, where zoning loopholes are being or can be employed, ad-hoc strategies are being formalized, or city governments and/or residents are seeking or re-evaluating strategies to address demand for affordable home-ownership options. The following therefore represent a series of tests of the Starter Home* thesis: each metropolitan area has its own "cracks" whether spatial, regulatory, or some combination thereof, that can be used as an advantage in the housing market.

Renting is getting less and less affordable, especially in metro areas – in the 100 largest metro areas in the country, from 2001-2009: 41.2-48.7% of renters were paying more than 30% income, and 20.7-26.1% paying more than 50%.

When prohibitive lot and mortgage sizes squeeze a portion of the consumer class out of the housing market, they turn to renting or continue to rent beyond the point at which they would otherwise have purchased a home. This in turn makes the rental market less affordable for everyone, and at the bottom end of the affordability spectrum, more and more people are left without options.

fig. 016

Joint Center for Housing Studies of Harvard University, "Rental Market Stresses..." 2011

The Starter Home* uses metro-specific land-based opportunities as central to its functioning:

Each urban area has its own particular "cracks" – under-utilized or altogether ignored lot types or zoning designations that escape normative planning efforts and development models. Identifying under-utilized land in cities is a process that itself has to be treated on a case by case basis, and involves an analysis of relative potentials. As a financial model, this opportunism affords the ability to find resource-rich neighborhoods, the benefit of which is in its contribution both to the network-based planning scheme of the Starter Home* as well as the freedom and adaptability central to its architectural strategy.

In the pursuit of urban "cracks," the requirement of contiguous parcels is in many cases abandoned in favor of the potential offered by a dispersed development – each parcel becomes part of an active whole, and the model of compensatory costs that applies in cases of normatively planned developments is applied across phases, requiring the integration of development and design interests.

A 2001 survey of 83 cities across the U.S. found that on average, 15% of a given city's land was vacant – whether due to contamination, location, irregular shape, size, or disinvestment.

fig. 017

**Ann O'M Bowman and Michael A. Pagano,
"Vacant Land in Cities: An Urban Resource"**

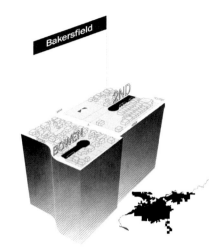

Bakersfield's downtown cul de sacs represent a
significant, and growing, urban street type with built-in
underutilized spaces. As the city continues to allow
developers to build cul de sacs in dense downtown
neighborhoods, there is opportunity to couple
Starter Home* development with normative housing
development.

Austin's creeks and streams flow through backyards,
parks, highways and empty lots across the city. Running
alongside them are buffer zones – undevelopable land
in an ownership limbo that could be exploited for the
production of housing stock.

New Orleans' urban form, guided by the Mississippi and attitudes towards planning at the time of its initial development, leaves under-sized, according to normative zoning regulations, non-conforming lots that remain undeveloped. Their potential use is as a dispersed, networked development, the elements of which can be inserted in neighborhoods across the city.

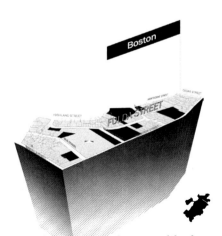

Boston's downtown – seemingly overrun and therefore devoid of development opportunities – has an un-used and un-recognized but robust supply of lots, owned and managed by the city and in many cases unattractive to downtown commercial developers.

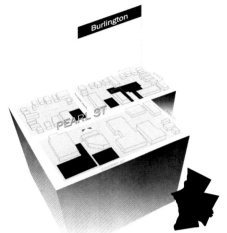

Abundant parking lots in downtown Burlington are becoming obsolete as the city government invests heavily in public transportation and restricts auto access in the downtown. Demand is high for residential and commercial development, making parking lots an emerging potential in the city.

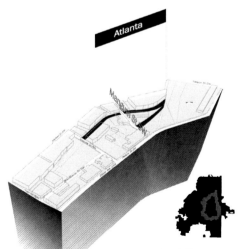

In 1970, the Atlanta City Council abandoned all city alleyways except for 3. Most are <10 feet wide. Ownership automatically transferred to adjacent property owners, who have the opportunity to restrict access and forego maintenance, leaving alleys entirely unused.

Interiority & Exteriority

Infill

Small unit types allow development to more easily fit into existing urban neighborhoods – rich sources of amenities that support a smaller home's functioning. In turn, greater density supports urban amenities, creating neighborhoods with greater bargaining power, larger tax bases, and more robust social networks.

Scale

The relatively consistent construction costs that help to dictate a home's sale price are mitigated when smaller footprints are embraced; moreover, maintenance and heating & cooling costs are lowered, creating a model of home ownership that is made more accessible across all major cost categories. At the scale of the block, the neighborhood, and the metro area, dense urban infill with smaller units allows for community wide sharing of infrastructure, support for economic networks, and shared participation in public systems – political, educational, social.

Material

The traditional model of affordable home delivery typically achieves a lower price point by adapting a standard market rate home on a typical lot alongside market rate homes, with lower cost versions of labor and materials, whether by donation or cheaper specifications. This model is limited by the typical house and lot size; achieving market-rate scale and amenities will always be constrained by the increasing costs associated with larger lots and occupiable square footage. Seeking cost savings in cheaper, lower quality materials and labor often leads to lower overall construction quality, which deteriorates standard of living, increases maintenance costs, and devalues a homeowner's investment over time.

Construction costs accounted for nearly 60% of the total sales price, including land costs, for the average new home built in 2011; this rate has remained relatively stable since 1998, with the greatest changes in average price-per-square-foot being attributable to variations in average lot sizes per year.

Efficiency improves quality

Small house movements have been in the fringes of the Starter Home conversation – appearing and fading into the background periodically over the 20th and 21st centuries. Figure 013 shows a design from the Architects' Small House Bureau, est. 1914, which purposed pro-domesticity rhetoric towards more affordable ends.

fig. 018

The Providence, RI Metro Area, 2011

"The Bureau has endeavored also to eliminate from its service all those types which the architect looks upon as ephemeral. The Bureau could no doubt sell a vastly larger number of working drawings if they were designed to meet popular taste, but there is no tendency on its part to waste its opportunity to advance the cause of the architect for the sake of making money. The houses are intended to be sound from every architectural point of view."

Metro areas are more affordable

Population shifts and the absorption of previously peripheral areas has reinvigorated the need to apply the starter home model to metro infill. The supply of vacant land in urban areas, often maligned but too quickly dismissed for its idiosyncrasies according to the perspective of the normative developer, makes metro infill a powerful if suprising potential area for investment.

"A Little Kingdom of Your Own...Small in Size but Large in the Resources of Home Making"

Ownership encourages mobility

Privileging a financial mobility over physical mobility is to reconsider the home-ownership paradigm: the question as to whether or not home ownership is key to the ideology of the American Dream has too frequently reduced the argument to a simple dualism.

fig. 019

NAHB, "New Construction Cost Breakdown" 2011

fig. 020

100 Bungalows of Frame and Masonry Construction, 1929, Architects' Small House Bureau

fig. 021

"The Architects' Small House Service Bureau," Architectural Forum 44, 1926

Network & Node

Resources

Where mid-century suburban development looked inward to amenities at the scale of the individual home – more and larger rooms, high-end fixtures and finishes, yards, storage space, multi-car garages – urban development turns outward toward amenities in the urban environment – schools, parks, transit and food networks, etc..

Access

Just as adjacent highway access does in the suburbs, dense urban neighborhoods provide easy and equitable access to shops, jobs, and schools, facilitating collective ownership and value that extends from the scale of the metro area to that of the individual property. As compared to traditional suburban support shops, schools, and highways, urban networks can be established piece-meal, and do not require great lobbying effort or developer capital to create.

Investment

Traditional mortgage lending and suburban development foreground the benefits of individual financial gain with personal investment and private ownership; with this individual benefit comes individual risk and responsibility – loss of value, rising interest rates, and building maintenance are borne by the individual home owner alone, who does not benefit from the effects of collective ownership, maintenance and value that exist in dense metro areas.

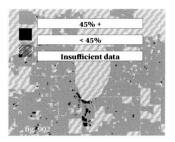

The cost of transportation is the second largest household expenditure after housing: costs fall between <10% and 25%, depending on location, access to transit options, and proximity to amenities; where a household falls on the spectrum affects what they can afford in terms of housing.

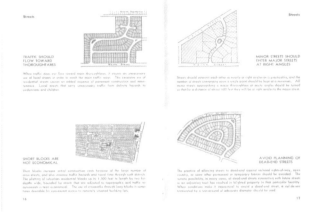

fig. 022 & 023

Map showing housing affordability in the Chicago Metro Area, incorporating transportation costs. Data from the census, as processed by the Center for Neighborhood Technology's H&T Index.

Rather than using 28% of income as an upper limit in mortgage calculation (as is the custom in standard loan underwriting), Location Efficient Mortgages allow borrowers up to 39%, as dictated by the transportation options available in their area.

The graphic above, using a sample family of 2.73 people, with 1.23 commuting workers, and an income of $60,289 (as is the average in the Chicago-Naperville-Joliet Metropolitan Statistical Area), shows that mortgage affordability is inverted relative to location when transportation accessibility is factored in to the calculation.

fig. 024

Brookings Institute, "Affordability Index" 2008

fig. 025

Alex Maclean, "Las Vegas and Venice from the Air" 2010

fig. 026

Spread from "Successful Subdivisions" 1940

Mobility

Equity

Equity in a home is a powerful bargaining chip that can offer homeowners the ability to relieve themselves of debt, open businesses, or alter career paths without worrying about one of their most essential concerns.

Stability

The number of cost-burdened households in America has risen precipitously – 40.9 million, or more than 1/3 of Americans are paying more than 30% of their income for housing (2012, up 9 million from 2009); among homeowners, on the other hand, the number of cost burdened houseolds is falling slowly – from 22 mil to 20.3 (2011-2012). Home ownership, when the scope of the home is kept within a household's income, can offer powerful stability.

Choice

Affordable housing – rental and ownership – are needed in metro areas across the United States; while efforts to regulate and incentivize incorporating affordable rental units into market rate buildings in desirable urban neighborhoods are picking up some steam, little attention is paid to the impressive roster of short and long-term benefits that could be afforded to an entry-level potential home-owner were they able

to buy into similarly desirable neighborhoods: access to better schools, more robust food and transportation networks, and the kinds of returns on investments that can be expected in areas with urban-scale services. Moreover, creating more accessible opportunities for home ownership in areas with rising home and rental prices can afford existing residents the ability to maintain a stake in their neighborhood while experiencing the benefits of a densifying community.

Home ownership benefits the individual owner and the broader economy; for the owner, a home is a tax shelter: the deduction of mortgage interest payments and that potential implicit rental income is un-taxed are two incentives.

In the 100 largest U.S. metro areas, housing costs 2.4 times more when located near to a high-scoring public school than a low-scoring school – the national average is an extra 11,000 per year.

PROVIDE SCHOOL
AND CHURCH SITES

1. School, playground; 2. Churches; 3. Business center

If a subdivision is large enough to warrant the consideration of all community requirements, locations should be provided for schools and churches. These sites should be centrally located for the convenience of all property owners and citizens in the vicinity.   Adequate space should be provided for the parking of automobiles, without interfering with residential property near the school and church.

13

fig. 029

Brookings Institute, "Housing Costs, Zoning, and Access to High-Scoring Schools" 2012

"In their seminal research developing a hedonic model for the prediction of house prices, Kain and Quigley (1970) included structural characteristics of the housing unit, neighborhood characteristics, and distance to the CBD. Reviews of hedonic models (Bowen et al. 2001; Malpezzi 2003) have described such models as including housing structure characteristics, the social and natural environment (neighborhood characteristics), and location within the market."

fig. 027

John R. Ottensman, Seth Payton, and Joyce Man, "Urban Location and Housing Prices within a Hedonic Model"

Young adults (18-34 years old) move more often than other age group - to follow jobs, find ideal neighborhoods or cities, etc. - but moving rates drop sharply in the early thirties (from 27% 20-24 to 14% 30-34) ; residential stability can either be achieved through staying in a rental unit for multiple years, or purchasing a home. The starter home model has always been designed with the young family in mind, because they represent the largest untapped market within the broader home consumption class.

fig. 028

Satyajit Chatterjee, "Taxes, Home Ownership, and the Allocation of Residential Real Estate Risks"

fig. 030

Spread from "Successful Subdivisions" 1940

fig. 031

U.S. Census Bureau, "Housing Characteristics: 2010"

The Starter Home*

Strategy & Form

fig. 032

**Carmelitos, California 1939, Housing
Authority of the City of Los Angeles and
Clarence S. Stein**

The starter home legacy

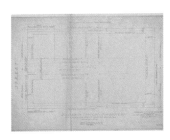

fig. 034

"A town for the motor age": Radburn, NJ 1929, Planning: Clarence S. Stein & Henry Wright, Landscape: Marjorie Sewell Cautley

fig. 035

Clarence Stein and the Carmelitos architects, 1938

fig. 036

"Preliminary Study of Two Super Blocks in Radburn, NJ" 1927, Clarence S. Stein & Henry Wright

From house, to housing, to planning

The American home has progressively accumulated interior resources; electrification, accessibility of appliances and the introduction of convenience-based amenities into the home have worked together with an ethos of autonomy and self-sufficiency [citation] to create an expectation that the home owner should find everything he or she needs in the home, as opposed to relying on resources outside of the home. As residential development in the 20th and 21st centuries has focused more on cheaper, suburban and exurban land, and lots and homes got larger, the home owner's ability to withdraw from the public sphere was nurtured.

In order to understand the contemporary expression of the Starter Home, it's important to consider the initial formation of the Starter Home model in the context of development pressures, homeowner expectations and technological advancements during the time when the American zoning code was initially designed. In 1916, the Standard Zoning Enabling Act was signed into law in New York City by then Mayor John Purroy Mitchel; it was the construction of the 38-story, 538' tall Equitable Building in the financial district in 1914, which towered over its neighbors, including Trinity Church (built in 1846, standing 284í at the tip of its spire), that sparked momentum behind codifying zoning regulations. By the end of 1916, eight cities had zoning codes. In 1926, the Supreme Court upheld zoning's constitutionality in Euclid v. Ambler, and though the case focused on industrial development in a residential area, the majority

opinion focused briefly on the "parasitic" action of multi-family housing in single-family residential neighborhoods; Justice George Sutherland wrote that apartments are "a mere parasite, constructed in order to take advantage of the open spaces and attractive surroundings created by the residential character of the district." (272 U.S. 394)

Zoning's rise to prominence as a means of land regulation in the United States followed the spread of electric rail through cities, which allowed those who could afford the transportation costs to move out of city centers and into newly forming residential "streetcar suburbs."

Subdivision at a relatively small scale engendered fairly homogenous neighborhoods without the aid of zoning; a combination of neighborhood pressure, and the fact that heavy industry still had to be aligned to freight rail and ports meant that streetcar suburbs could maintain their homogeneity without zoning. When trucking became a viable alternative for heavy industry, manufacturers could buy and develop land wherever they wanted, and

fig. 037

Interstate Power Company advertisement
1946

fig. 038

Park Forest, Illinois 1952

fig. 039

Cover of "Toward New Towns for America"
1966, Clarence S. Stein

industry began to infringe upon residential neighborhoods. Similarly, once buses began to replace streetcars as the primary form of transport for apartment dwellers, apartment developers were no longer beholden to the streetcar line and could buy land in previously homogenous single-family-detached areas. The relative profitability of industrial and multi-family development compared with single-family detached meant that no amount of neighborhood pressure could prevent the sale of land to developers looking to profit from bringing new uses into neighborhoods. In part from the resistance of homeowners to changing neighborhood demographics came the campaign for zoning regulation.

It was primarily the protection of home values driving the argument for zoning. Eventually, it was the developers of large-scale subdivisions who became some of the most vocal supporters of zoning, as the same "economy of scale" argument that drives development today was made possible through economic, legal, and technological changes in the building industry. Subdivision of ever-larger tracts of land became the key to bringing the interests of developers and the interests of homeowners together.

From house, to housing, to planning: consumption and progress

Residential subdivision in America was therefore originally a fundamentally wealthy, suburban phenomenon; by the 1920s, with zoning regulations in place, legal deed restriction, and the expansion of multi-modal transport networks, developers used large-scale lot subdivision to create uniform neighborhoods according to the principle that home value stability and overall development profitability would benefit the larger the development.

> *"The more I think of what has been happening in the field of housing in this country during the last decade the more strongly I feel that the essential lack has been our inability to see that the house itself is of minor importance. Its relation to the community is the thing that really counts...It is not only the fact that a small house must depend on its grouping with other houses for its beauty, and for the preservation of light, air,*

and the maximum of surrounding open space. What is probably more important is the economic angle. It is impossible to build homes according to the American standard as individual units for those of limited incomes. If they are to be soundly built and completely equipped with the essential utilities they must be planned and constructed as part of a larger group."

Clarence Stein, 1930

It wasn't until the post-WWII suburban housing boom that the development process graduated from one divided into land acquisition, subdivision and improvement on one hand, and home building and sale on the other, to a vertically integrated process wherein all parts of the process were controlled by one party or company. Mass production in the building industry was essential to this integration, and the incorporation of amenities – retail, schools, open space, etc. – became a major selling point to the young families who made up the majority of new, first-time home buyers at the time. Starter Home developers, at this point, embraced planning as a tool, along with zoning, to increase profitability at the same time as the architectural community was embracing planning as the new frontier of practice. In 1940, the Federal Housing Authority published "Successful Subdivisions", codifying the design principles developed by the past generations' residential developers.

fig. 040

SOM's "aton bomb city" in Oak Ridge, TN 1949

Architects as planners:

In 1943, Architectural Forum invited a group of architects to imagine the post-war American city, and to propose a relationship between architecture and planning; they used the term "194X" to describe the future, as yet unknown, year that the war would end, to organize the group of invited architects, and to convey the inchoate attitude towards the urban scale in the field of architecture. The rhetoric stemming from the architects in 194X, as well as within the broader field, was, in fact, already enmeshed in the

Something infinitely more serious than a new fad.

fig. 041

Illustration from "A Crack in the Picture Window" 1956, John Keats

"For literally nothing down—other than a simple two percent and a promise to pay, and pay, and pay until the end of your life—you too, like a man I'm going to call John Drone, can find a box of your own in one of the fresh-air slums we're building around the edges of America's cities."

fig. 042

"Mr. Blandings Builds His Dream House"
1948, Adaptation of Eric Hodgins' 1946
novel by the same name.

fig. 043

Still from Martha Rosler's "Semiotics of
the Kitchen" 1975

"An anti-Julia Child replaces the
domesticated `meaning' of tools with a
lexicon of rage and frustration."

commercial world of community planning. No longer was it only the domestic sphere that inspired consumption patterns or the self-reflective building that held the focus of designers' rhetoric – the shift towards urban design within the field of architecture, partially in response to the historically problematic relationship between architecture and planning and partially fed by the social consciousness of the modern architects of the 1920s and 30s, was matched by the capital thrust of the building industry. This confluence of industry, interest and finance married progressive architectural desires to big business, specifically the big business of community planning, and created a formidable opponent to publicly funded planning projects.

Embedded ideologies: refining the model, defining expectations:

It is not only the physical manifestations of the starter home over the course of the 20th and 21st centuries in America that are crucial to understanding the broader starter home phenomenon, but also the rhetorical shifts that have accompanied formal, urbanistic, and technological changes in the domestic landscape. A critique of the starter home within popular culture began in earnest as early as the 1940s, coinciding with the boom in the construction industry that accompanied the shift of war-time production capacities to the starter home industry at the close of WWII. Just as advertising campaigns began to propagandize the properly designed and inhabited domestic environment as the ultimate patriotic victory, domesticity was in turn problematized in intellectual, academic, and cultural circles.

fig. 044

"The Money Pit" 1986, Remake of "Mr.
Blandings" with Tom Hanks and Shelley
Long

fig. 045

A.J. Davis' "English Villa: in the Rustic Cottage Style"

" I long for the preservation of those pure, simple, holy tastes, which have led our countrymen, in all ages, to delight in the... profound peace of noble woods."

fig. 048

Harwell Hamilton Harris Architects, 1946 Harris Libbey Owens Glass Co. housing competition winner.

"Thanks to glass, light, like space, has become a flexible element of design."

fig. 051

Levitt & Sons' Cambridge Park advertisement, 1970

"For value conscious families who want a home right away!"

fig. 046

Sears' Modern Homes Catalog 1911, Sears Robuck and Co.

"Somewhere in these pages is a design which peculiarly expresses your individuality."

fig. 049

"Bill Levitt's Third Big Town" 1958, House and Home Magazine

"You can't have houses without schools"

fig. 052

Life's Dream House issue, 1994

"A house that's classic on the outside, remarkable on the inside, and affordable. It can be adapted to suit your family, and can be built anywhere you want."

fig. 047

100 Bungalows of Frame and Masonry Construction, 1929, Architects' Small House Service Bureau

Simplicity implies character, quality and taste. Simplicity implies cheerfulness, happiness, prosperity, and light."

fig. 050

"A Wonderful World of Your Own" 1959, Eichler Homes

"Don't underestimate the importance of your surroundings when you serve meals to your family and friends."

"An exciting exploration into future living!"

fig. 053

Pulte Homes' "Arts District Hyattsville"

"The best place to live in D.C. isn't in D.C.: immerse yourself in a community that embraces the art of city living."

The Starter Home*

*Rhetorical shifts reflect changing
attitudes toward domesticity...*

fig. 054

**Martha Rosler's "Cleaning the Drapes"
from "Bringing the War Home: House
Beautiful," 1967-1972**

1907

A Fireproof House for $5000

Living Space	1186 sq ft
# Rooms	10
Price	$5,000
Type	Frank Lloyd Wright's Ladies Home Journal house

1911

Modern Home no. 165

Living Space	1580 sq ft
# Rooms	6
Price	$1,362
Type	Sears Robuck catalog house

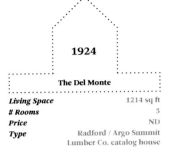

1924

The Del Monte

Living Space	1214 sq ft
# Rooms	5
Price	ND
Type	Radford / Argo Summit Lumber Co. catalog house

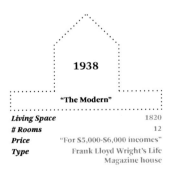

1924

The Dixon

Living Space	1960 sq ft
# Rooms	12
Price	ND
Type	Radford catalog house

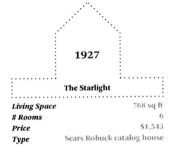

1927

The Starlight

Living Space	768 sq ft
# Rooms	6
Price	$1,543
Type	Sears Robuck catalog house

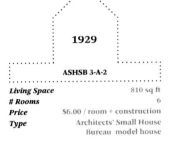

1929

ASHSB 3-A-2

Living Space	810 sq ft
# Rooms	6
Price	$6.00 / room + construction
Type	Architects' Small House Bureau model house

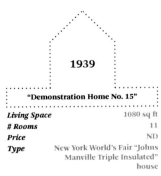

1938

"The Modern"

Living Space	1820
# Rooms	12
Price	"For $5,000-$6,000 incomes"
Type	Frank Lloyd Wright's Life Magazine house

1939

"Demonstration Home No. 15"

Living Space	1080 sq ft
# Rooms	11
Price	ND
Type	New York World's Fair "Johns Manville Triple Insulated" house

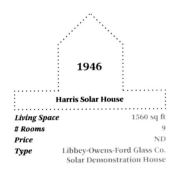

1946

Harris Solar House

Living Space	1560 sq ft
# Rooms	9
Price	ND
Type	Libbey-Owens-Ford Glass Co. Solar Demonstration House

1955

"Prairie Fields"

Living Space	1072 sq ft
# Rooms	8
Price	ND
Type	Cliff May's "Magazine Cover Home" Series House

1958

"Storybook"

Living Space	1,419 sq ft
# Rooms	9
Price	$11,990
Type	Levittown, NJ house

1960

"Stone and Shingle"

Living Space	2,170 sq ft
# Rooms	12
Price	$20,990
Type	Levittown, MA house

1961

Plan 1544

Living Space	1741 sq ft
# Rooms	11
Price	ND
Type	Eichler Homes Catalog

1971

The Salem

Living Space	2,200
# Rooms	12
Price	$28,990
Type	Levitt & Sons Cambridge Park Development

1980

Kite Hill Contemporary

Living Space	2,320
# Rooms	12
Price	$30,700
Type	Shappell / S&S Homes

1994

Chadwick Bay

Living Space	2,440
# Rooms	12
Price	$1500 Plans Only
Type	Home Planners "Small House"

2001

Covington Cottage

Living Space	1941
# Rooms	12
Price	$930 Plans Only
Type	Souther Living Dream House

2007

DHSW67493

Living Space	2,553
# Rooms	13
Price	$1,100 Plans Only
Type	Dream Home Source

Beyond the prototype

Strategic infill matches development model to design.

The starter home* that we are developing is not a prototype; rather, it is designed to function as a holistic strategy that embraces site-specific spatial and economic conditions; its architectural expression is generated equally in response to market and regulatory forces as it is to design intent and ideas about the domestic sphere.

At the same time, our starter home* does not belong in a green-field, planned community development. Relying on the amenities that are built into metro areas allows our starter homes* to be efficient, just as it requires them to be strategic, and participatory: their relationship to their context, at the scale of the site, the neighborhood, and the metropolitan region, is a primary driver of design. Moreover, each individual starter home*, even as it is situated on its particular site, also functions within the group of starter homes*: it is a dispersed development.

Important to the starter home* thesis is the idea that construction costs can be mitigated while maintaining a high quality product by reducing the burden of associated costs – maintenance costs, land costs, material costs – and emphasizing site sensitivity over rote reproducibility. This is where a new kind of economy-of-scale becomes necessary: one that requires integration of design and development interests, agility, and the ability to accommodate changes in each project's matrix of preconditions, drivers, goals and resources.

Ownership bolsters the market

A generation of would-be first time home buyers are waiting longer to buy into the market than their analogues in previous generations– combined with levels of student loan debt, the lasting effects of the recession on the job market, and an increasingly cautious attitude towards investing, the percentage of people entering the homeownership market vs. continuing to rent as they enter their late twenties through thirties is decreasing, even as these renters start having families, find stable jobs, and stop moving as often.

Homes can rebuild credit

When the housing bubble burst in 2008, it became apparent that many people had been given the opportunity to buy "too much house" - in the wake of foreclosure, one way to re-enter the housing market (and rebuild credit) is through the purchase of small mortgages with short terms.

Greater breadth adds stability

According to the Harvard Joint Center for Housing Studies' "Where Can Renters Afford to Own?" interactive map, 44.7% of renters age 25-34 can afford to own a home in New Orleans, whereas the actual home-ownership rate among 25-34 year olds is 36.6%. The overall home ownership rate in New Orleans is 61.3%, the median income for 25-34 year olds is $30,439, and the median home price is $164,150 for which monthly owner costs would be $950.

fig. 055

Harvard Joint Center for Housing Studies, "Where Can Renters Afford to Own?" Interactive Map, 2014

fig. 056

Drawing for Truss Wall House 1992, Ushida Findlay Architects

In the 1990s, Japan entered a recession that affected the construction industry and guided many architects, trained during the boom, towards collaborative design collectives and small, urban infill projects. Consumers, too, were attracted more to metro areas than suburbs for purchasing opportunities. The result is an architectural tradition of highly formally experimental, small, one-off single family homes in Japan's most densely populated cities.

The Starter Home* is not a prototype

Neither is it a formal exercise, designed for hyper-specified or prescribed inhabitation – our purpose here is to create an architectural mode rather than model, one that is as responsive as it is democratic.

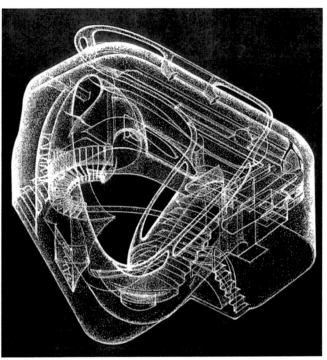

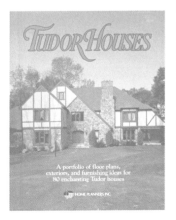

fig. 057

Home Planners Inc. Portfolio, 1994

In the 1970s, regional neo-eclecticism rose to prominence in the American new-construction residential market. The application of style gave the consumer a sense of empowerment through customization.

Choice has always been central to the single-family, and by extension starter, home industry – whether implied via superficially applied architectural style or complete customization according to novel and/or projective modes of inhabitation, the ability to express individuality through the home is a major driver of consumption. In either case re-sale is complicated, on the one hand by the presumption that stylistic difference can supplant programmatic flexibility, and on the other by particularity.

Whether from a catalog, or as part of a comprehensive planned community, relying on infill or large lot subdivision, made up of private homes, or including community amenities,

Greenbelt, Maryland
1937

Forest Hills Gardens
1909

Radburn, New Jersey
1929

Windsor, Denver
1970

San Mateo Highlands
1956-1964

starter homes share a mutual genesis as responses to a need for housing, the desire to attract new consumers to the market, and an aspiration to participate in the typology's evolution.

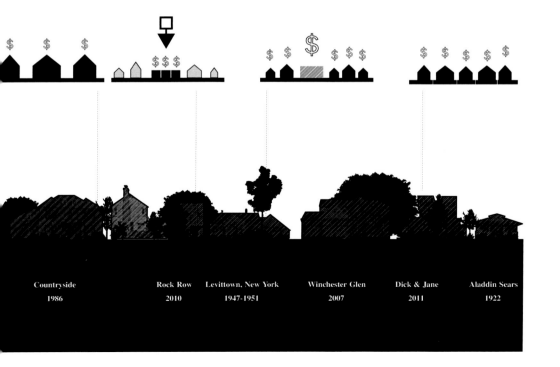

Countryside
1986

Rock Row
2010

Levittown, New York
1947-1951

Winchester Glen
2007

Dick & Jane
2011

Aladdin Sears
1922

The Starter Home*

Place and Placelessness

fig. 058

**James Casabere's "Landscape with Houses",
2011**

Typological Vocabularies

fig. 059

Gerald Rupp A-frame, 1949, Morro Bay California

Adjustments and associations

In the 1950s the a-frame was the expression of a coalescence of two major ideological / socio-economic forces in America: the technologically-supported polarization of work and play, and the middle-class aspiration, generated by the post-war boom, that encouraged people to expect that after home ownership came, naturally, second-home-ownership.

These leisure houses were fantasies, both for the user and the architect – the restrictions of every-day life and every-day design were abandoned in favor of exuberant geometries, as well as the built-in impracticalities that went along with the new forms. Freed from the pressure to view the home as useful in the conventional, every-day sense, consumers were more likely to take risks and embrace programmatic, technological, spatial, and aesthetic innovations.

fig. 060

Douglas Fir Plywood Association Plan Book

Significantly, because this new second-home market had a very particular audience – the burgeoning middle class – economy was essential. The dream of owning a vacation home, newly available to a much broader audience, could only survive if it were actually accessible; the building industry, in turn, could benefit from a new income stream only if it were able to speak to the particular aspirations of the moment while achieving the right price point.

Because of this, formal experimentation became inseparable from affordability.

fig. 061

John Campbell A-frame, 1951, San Francisco California

fig. 062

Elizabeth Reese House 1995, Andrew Geller

The a-frame, as a device, has an ancient history: the simplicity of its constructibility and efficiency in building material use have made it attractive as a building strategy across the world. Post-WWII in the United States, the a-frame had a resurgence, for the most part for precisely the same utilitarian reasons as had given it its place in history as a traditional building type. As wartime production capacities were reoriented towards post-war industries – the building industry foremost among them – introducing the burgeoning middle class to the second-home market became a major economic driver, and the a-frame was poised to provide consumers with an affordable option with a strong identity.

No sooner did the a-frame's efficiencies, and inefficiencies, surge to prominence in 20th century America did it begin to inspire experiments with other simple geometric forms. Often "leisure homes," they housed the optimism, aspirations and fears of the Cold War era.

fig. 064

Rendering of Geller's "Leisurama House" – sold fully furnished by Macy's

fig. 063

Andrew Geller's Pearlroth, or "Double Diamond" House, 1958

fig. 063

Henrik Bull's Klaussen Cabin, 1954, Squaw Valley

The absolutism of the a-frame makes it perfectly suitable for modification...

A-frame manipulations: formal operations

The geometry of the a-frame is both highly distinctive, in its unmediated form, and highly responsive to pressures; manipulations of type that rely on simple applications of design modifications can use the potential of the a-frame, structurally and in its material efficiency, while overcoming its typological associations, and the, in some cases, overly simplistic formal expression of its unmodified form.

Manipulation of type:

01. *Sectional geometry*

02. *% Compliance*

03. *Core location*

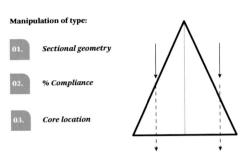

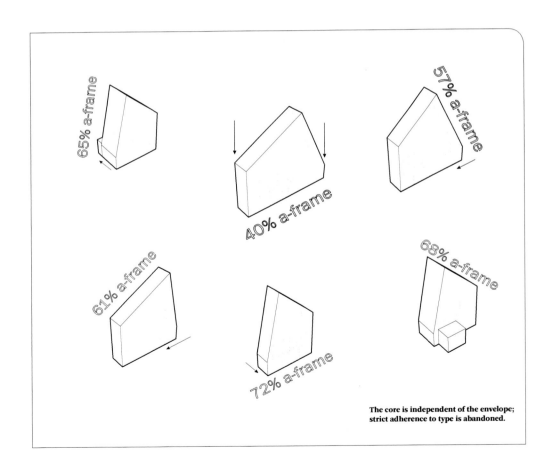

The core is independent of the envelope; strict adherence to type is abandoned.

Manipulation of type:

01. *Relative width*

02. *Relative height*

03. *Wall thickness*

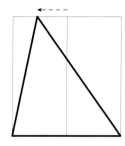

In both its modified and unmodified form, the a-frame has a number of built-in inefficiencies, especially with respect to interior occupiable square footage. This can be addressed in a number of ways, the first of which involves assessing the potential for doubling up of uses; in the same way as the roof and wall systems overlap, program can be built into structure, creating opportunity from loss of usefulness.

BUILT-IN
UN-OCCUPIABLE
SPACE

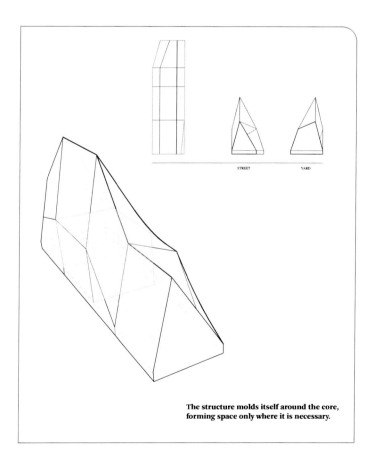

STREET   YARD

The structure molds itself around the core,
forming space only where it is necessary.

MORE OCCUPIABLE SPACE

LESS OCCUPIABLE SPACE

BUILT-IN
STORAGE

A-frame manipulations: figure & ground

Expansion / contraction

Subtraction

Division

Relative angle

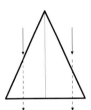

One of the powerful things about the a-frame, as a device, is in its ability to remain in the realm of the diagram. Embracing this quality while introducing consequent design drivers allows us to begin to "site" the otherwise placeless form.

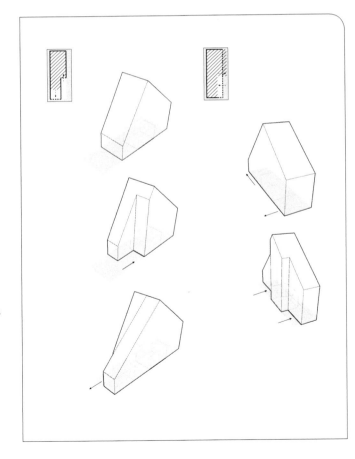

Restricting ourselves to a
few simple operations allows
us to begin to consider the
role of an operative logic
in a series of architectural
expressions that, though not
identical, must maintain
a familial, evolutionary
relationship to one another.
In this sense, the economy
of the reproducible starter
home is brought in to the
design exercise in mediated
form.

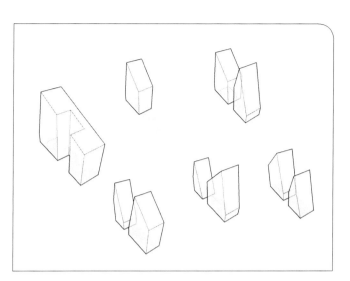

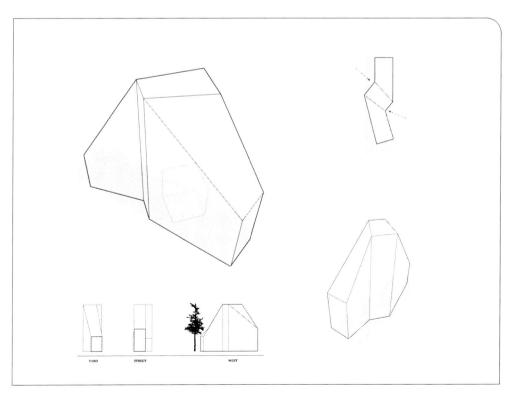

YARD   STREET   WEST

A-frame manipulations: figure & ground

Expansion / contraction

Subtraction

Division

Relative angle

A shifting centerline can begin to foresee responses to internal needs – spatial, programmatic – and external needs – environmental, circulatory, etc.

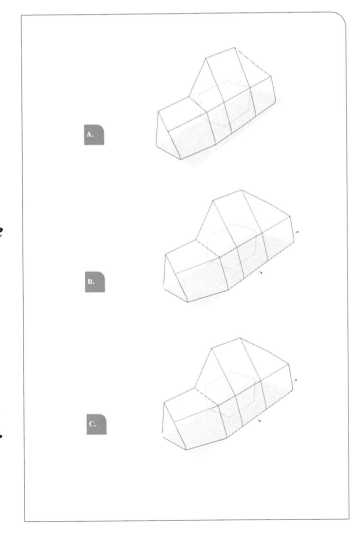

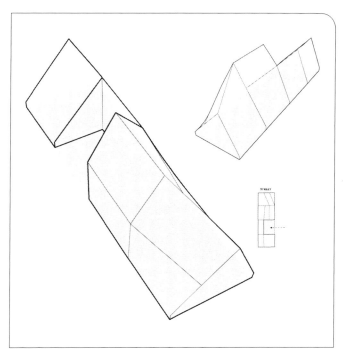

"Stacking" operations introduces formal complexity and ensures enough flexibility to address any site requirements presented upon siting.

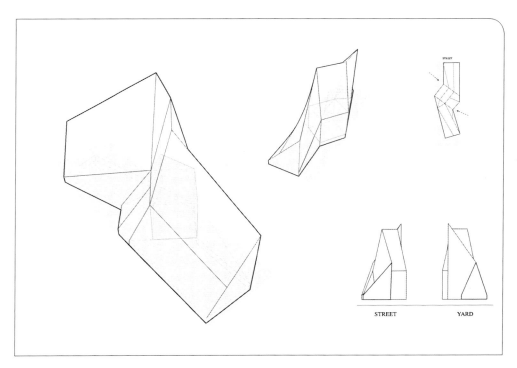

The Starter Home*

References & Works consulted

Adler, Margot. "Behind the Ever-Expanding American Dream House." National Public Radio, July 4, 2006, sec. All Things Considered.

Albrecht, Donald. World War II and the American Dream: How Wartime Building Changed a Nation. MIT Press, 1994.

Altman, Karen E. "Consuming Ideology: The Better Homes in America Campaign." Critical Studies in Mass Communication 7 (1990): 286–307.

American Planning Association. Modernizing State Planning Statutes. The Growing Smart Working Papers 462/463, 1996.

"Architects' Small House Service Bureau ASHSB Records," n.d. Minnesota Historical Society.

Arnold, Chris. "Sluggish Housing Market a Product of Millions of 'Missing Households.'" National Public Radio, June 18, 2014.

Belsky, Eric S., Christopher E. Herbert, and Jennifer H. Molinsky. Homeownership Built to Last: Balancing Access, Affordability, and Risk after the Housing Crisis. Washington, D.C.: The Brookings Institution, 2014.

Belsky, Eric S, Michael Schill, and Anthony Yezer. "The Effect of the Community Reinvestment Act on Bank and Thrift Home Purchase Mortgage Lending." Joint Center for Housing Studies: Harvard University, August 2001.

Benjamin, Richard. The Money Pit, 1986.

Bennett, Donna S. "Condominium Homeownership in the United States: A Selected Annotated Bibliography of Legal Sources." Law Library Journal 103, no. 2 (n.d.): 2011–16.

Boustan, Leah P., and Robert A. Margo. "A Silver Lining to White Flight? White Suburbanization and African-American Homeownership, 1940-1980." Journal of Urban Economics 78 (2013): 71–80.

Bowman, Ann, and Michael A. Pagano. Terra Incognita: Vacant Land and Urban Strategies. Georgetown University Press, 2010.

———. "Vacant Land in Cities: An Urban Resource." The Brookings Institution, n.d.

Callis, Robert R, and Melissa Kresin. "Residential Vacancies and Homeownership in the First Quarter 2014." U.S. Dept. of Commerce: Social, Economic, and Housing Statistics Division, April 2014.

Center for Transit-Oriented Development, and Center for Neighborhood Technology. "The Affordability Index: A New Tool for Measuring the True Affordability of a Housing Choice." The Brookings Institution Metropolitan Policy Program Urban Markets Initiative, n.d.

Colton, Kent W. Housing in the Twenty-First Century: Achieving Common Ground. Wertheim Publications in Industrial Relations. Harvard University Press, 2003.

Dietz, Robert, and Natalia Siniavskaia. "The Geography of Home Size and Occupancy." National Association of Home Builders, n.d.

Easterling, Keller. Organization Space: Landscapes, Highways, and Houses in America. MIT Press, 2001.

Ehrenhalt, Alan. The Great Inversion and the Future of the American City. New York: Random House, 2013.

Emrath, Paul. "Characteristics of Homes Started in 2012: Size Increase Continues." National Association of Home Builders, 2013.

Fischel, William A. "An Economic History of Zoning and a Cure for Its Exclusionary Effects." Dartmouth College, December 2001.

Frederick, Christine. Selling Mrs. Consumer, n.d.

Glaeser, Edward L. "Rethinking the Federal Bias Toward Homeownership." Cityscape: A Journal of Policy Development and Research 13, no. 2 (2011): 5–37.

Grebler, Leo, David M. Blank, and Louis Winnick. Capital Formation in Residential Real Estate: Trends and Prospects. Princeton University Press, 1956.

Hartman, Chester, and Robin Drayer. "Military-Family Housing: The Other Public-Housing Program." Housing and Society 17, no. 3 (1990).

Hillier, Amy E. "Who Received Loans? Home Owners' Loan Corporation Lending and Discrimination in Philadelphia in the 1930's." Journal of Planning History 2, no. 1 (2003): 3–24.

Hodgins, Eric. Mr. Blandings Builds His Dream House, 1946.

Joint Center for Housing Studies: Harvard University. "The State of the Nation's Housing: Housing Challenges," 2014.

Keller Easterling GSAPP. Call It Home: The House That Private Enterprise Built, n.d.

Kolko, Jed. "Why the Homeownership Rate Is Misleading." The New York Times, January 30, 2014.

Leichenko, Robin M. "Growth and Change in U.S. Cities and Suburbs." Growth and Change 32 (Summer 2001): 326–54.

"Median and Average Square Feet of Floor Area in New Single-Family Houses Completed by Location: 1973-2010." Census Bureau, n.d.

Metropolitan Policy Program. "State of Metropolitan America: On the Front Lines of Demographic Transformation." Brookings Institute, 2010.

Miller, Joshua J. "Snapshot of Home Ownership in Local Housing Markets." National Association of Home Builders, March 2014.

Piazzesi, Monika, Martin Schneider, and Selale Tuzel. "Housing, Consumption, and Asset Pricing." Journal of Financial Economics 83 (2007): 531–69.

Potter, H.C. Mr. Blandings Builds His Dream House, 1948.

Rosler, Martha. Semiotics of the Kitchen, 1975.

Sarkar, Mousumi. "Home American Homes Vary By the Year They Were Built." United States Census Bureau, June 2011.

Schwartz, Alex F. Housing Policy in the United States: An Introduction. New York: Routledge, 2006.

Shanken, Andrew M. 194X: Architecture, Planning, and Consumer Culture on the American Home Front. Minneapolis: University of Minnesota Press, 2009.

Shiller, Robert J. "Why Home Prices Change (or Don't)." The New York Times, April 13, 2013.

Taylor, Heather. "Cost of Constructing a Home." National Association of Home Builders, January 2014.

Twiss, Pamela, and James A. Martin. "Conventional and Military Public Housing for Families." Social Service Review 73, no. 2 (1999): 240–60.

US Census Bureau. "Housing Characteristics: 2010." U.S. Dept. of Commerce: Economics and Statistics Administration, October 2011.

———. "Measuring America: The Decennial Censuses From 1790 to 2000." U.S. Dept. of Commerce: Economics and Statistics Administration, September 2002.

U.S. Department of Housing and Urban Development. "2013 Characteristics of New Housing." U.S. Dept. of Commerce: Economics and Statistics Administration, n.d.

Weiss, Marc A. The Rise of the Community Builders: The American Real Estate Industry and Urban Land Planning. Beard Books, 2002.

What Works Collaborative. "Rental Market Stresses: Impacts of the Great Recession on Affordability and Multifamily Lending." Joint Center for Housing Studies: Harvard University, July 2011.

Woodstock Institute. "A Lifetime of Assets: Asset Preservation, Trends and Interventions in Asset Stripping Services and Products." National Community Reinvestment Coalition, n.d.

Wright, Gwendolyn. Building the Dream: A Social History of Housing in America. Cambridge: MIT Press, 1983.

Zhou, Yu, and Donald R. Haurin. "On the Determinants of House Value Volatility." JRER 32, no. 4 (2010).

fig. 064

**James Casabere's "Landscape with Houses",
2011**